Are We Seeing This?

by Mike Christie

Mike Christie

mikechristie.substack.com
ISBN 9781732320949
Cover design and art by Vanessa Swenson

Are We Seeing This?

For Emily.

For my parents.

And for all friends and family and the web
of support you make.

Thank you!

Mike Christie

Table of Contents

Mike Christie

Are We Seeing This?

There is a story in every thing, and every being, and every moment, were we alert to catch it, were we ready with our tender nets; indeed there are a hundred, a thousand stories, uncountable stories, could they only be lured out and appreciated; and more and more now I realize that what I thought was a skill only for authors and pastors and doctors and dream-diviners is the greatest of all human skills, the one that allows us into the heart and soul and deepest layers of our companions on the brief sunlit road between great dark wildernesses.

\- Brian Doyle

I don't know what a prayer is, but I do know how to pay attention.

\- Mary Oliver

Mike Christie

Forward

This is a book about stories that point up and out of themselves, a book about attention being the greatest of prayers, a book about categories melting into themes and themes swirling and splattering as if they were paint on a brush attached to the wings of a caffeinated goose flapping its wings…

You could say it is a book about trying to name something unnamable. But that seems a bit grandiose, does it not? Perhaps it is just leaning into hopeful possibility? Setting cynicism down for a moment? Jumping up and down in the middle of the walk around the neighborhood to be reminded that the body can move in many different ways?

There are poems here and there are essays and there are murmurings and there's a metaphorical bag of little seeds I've tried to pick up and hand to you and maybe they break open and maybe you see something in a new way?

This book asks the question, *Are We Seeing This?* "This" being the fact that we are here and there is *stuff* going on and underneath all that *stuff* there is a whole other dynamic at play. Like when you were a kid and you flipped over a garden rock and saw that wild world of bugs! I loved flipping over those rocks.

My hope is this is kind of like that.

I sense there's a lot right here and right now when we move away from naysaying and consider the world through a lens of wonder and curiosity. Still finding time to lean into the difficult and the pain. And in the balance of all that, discovering an intricate web shimmying toward confluence and connection. A harmony built on love and tenderness tying together each piece and part.

Are we seeing this?

Reach

More convinced now than ever
there is no necessity outside of reaching out.
Joint hands
with the universal
through the particular

Will you tell me what you love?
Here is mine
Boundless unfolding of who I am
and you are
to all the other pieces
parceled and placed
proximal and purposed

The name Divine
is a song webbed together with wonder
Binding and drawing us all toward the possibility
that we are capable of seeing
of being

Beauty and hope
Light and softness

Tenderly I reach
to all that bubbles before
Setting cynicism down

and running to that field
where you and I can tumble and twist
beyond our rights and wrongs
and into the arms of the all

Frog Sightings and Common Occurring Rarities

Have you ever experienced the absolute, sheer, uncorrupted, no-questions-asked joy that hits you square in the face like an egg shot from a sling-shot when you see a frog that you weren't expecting to?! There may be no greater event.

This happened the other day. I was on the back deck with my family at their house in Michigan and we were getting ready to leave for the airport. I had been visiting for about a week and was about to head home to my wife and dog—and the wonderful swirl that is *paving one's own path*—when all of a sudden, out of the somberness of departure, rose a gasp.

Look, a frog! My Mom said, joyously. Hopping across the deck was a little web-footed, midsummer-leaf-green colored, slimy-subtle creature.

Frogs are subtle, are they not? There's no flaunting, no pretense. There's a certain level of awkwardness that is tied to only being able to hop to get around, I'd imagine. Just think about that for a moment! *Hopping* around the grocery aisle, *hopping* down the aisle on your wedding day, *hopping* aboard a plane.

Everyone rushed to the spot on the deck where the frog had stopped. It looked up. We looked down. The dog came over — a lug of a golden retriever named Mowgli — he also bent down and met the frog eye-to-eye. The frog remained motionless. Eyes big. Looking ahead.

We were running late to the airport to begin with. There's something wonderful about thinking that I could have missed a flight on a plane flying 34,000 feet in the air and covering over 2,000 miles in under five hours, all of this …. due to a frog sighting.

Frogs are a common occurring rarity.

Think of the horror of being so ready and preoccupied with getting to the airport that you totally *missed the frog!* Hopefully, life never reaches that sinful state.

Common occurring rarities deserve our attention. They are the infinity of prayers shooting up from within the infinity of occurrences that make up what we call common, everyday life.

And it is my sense that the holy, *whatever* and *wherever* that word might be, is inviting us to a soft-furred nuzzle through our rapt attention to them.

We Are What We Were, and They Are, Too

The bug has six legs and is a pale green and is having a most difficult time navigating my arm hair and I have no idea its name.

This always seems to happen.

Sunny day, sitting outside—queue the insect friends. Landing on me as if I'm the local airport. Their layover long enough to make their presence known. My forearm being an airport bartender. Metaphor… digress.

It seems that humans rarely seek out such things, much less, tolerate them. Creepy-crawlys is what we've cleverly labeled our tiny (not always…) unfamiliar (our doing!) friends of infinite variety. Brushed off and blown away before we even take a second to really *see*.

Have you ever been still long enough to watch the lady bug's circular form open up as it lifts in flight? Does it register in the brain that the beady-black eyes of the grasshopper on the strawberry leaf are witnessing you, too?? Can you fathom how FAST those tiny little ant legs are pumping as they scurry across the sidewalk???

I know I rarely consider it.

There is a chance that somewhere along the timeline of our own physicality— at some point in the history of the matter that consists of us... you and me... right now — we were a queen ant!

Royalty and power quite unfamiliar to my normal human normalness.

What caries on with us when the breath of our lungs carries on no more? Where do we go when that happens? There are an infinite number of lives we've been before. What's next?

Is it possible the memory of those other lives is held by the world around us? That each bug landing on my skin remembers me as its own kind somewhere along the timeline?

Probably not, I hear you (and me, quite frankly) say. HOW BORING!

Maybe, simply, I as the human with the shallow and individualized memory that can only gather my life (and has fragmented that already beyond belief in only 27 minuscule years) can't see them for who they once were to the eternalized me?

I suppose there is no way to know. But the questions and the possibilities seem worthwhile enough reason to slow down the blow or swat each time they navigate the terrain of the skin I just so happen to hold now, in this moment along the timeline.

The Family

I have looked at leaves and slugs today
and I feeeeel the mustard.
The purpose behind the purposes we play,
The field beyond the fields we play.
There is so much family and symbiosis.

Will we ever fall fully into the family that's waiting?

Remembering My Grandfather

On the last flight of his life, my grandfather hadn't brought a book. He didn't fuss with a free headset to watch a movie or catch up with the news. Bewildered by what must have been over four hours of immense boredom, I asked him what he *had* done during the flight. He was coming to visit me, so I'd been on the same flight numerous times and I knew it's long and grueling and a bit boring even *with* a book or a show or some other distraction.

His answer was matter-of-fact: *I just looked out the window.*

If I were to boil down all my interactions with my grandpa into one lesson that I gleaned from him during the 25 years our existence coincided; it would be simple — *there is enough mystery in our midst to last our curiosity a lifetime.*

No matter the duration of our time spent together, inevitably at some point in the interaction he would raise his arms, get bug-eyed, and say *God* — in a way that sounded like *GOWHD!* — not out of any kind of deeply held reverence, but because there was no other word that seemed to capture what awe and wonder he was gleaning from where or what his mind was focused.

The stories are vast.

His eyes would wander out over the vast canopy of deciduous trees in my parents' backyard, following the paths of squirrels and other assorted creatures. He was completely detached from any conversation, and would only interject an occasional comment, making some reference to the world of wonder from which he had just returned.

There was the time when, with the greatest of detail, he told me about the rabbits in his backyard, with which he had a conflicted relationship. They had been eating his flowers, but he was intrigued somehow that they *knew* to come back to the *same* flower day after day. His own joy in seeing them consistently led him to make them a new offering: Cheerios, in a cereal bowl underneath some patio furniture. And standing by the sliding door, he would watch, calling to Grandma to gleefully announce the return of his friends the rabbits. Coming back, as he put it, "to stick their mug," in his offering bowl. *Now how does an animal know to come back like that? Think of the brain power. I mean, my GOWHD.*

Similar sentiments were expressed when I told him that fireflies didn't die in the winter, but burrowed underground, to which he went on a tear about resurrection, not mentioning our middle eastern Jewish buddy, Jesus, but instead choosing to focus on the resurrections *here and now*—the ones he witnessed every day of his life; through the fireflies out his window and the snakes and the bugs and the birds and the rabbits that seemingly always somehow came back to his gardens over the years. And beyond that, returning year after year, long after we pass.

His words, *his* choice of animals—not mine.

How do they know to return like that? He wondered aloud.

So where are you, Grandpa? Where has the 'you' of you wandered off to? Where, or perhaps how, do you return like these living things you marveled at? Surely you are doing so, because I know you would never have accepted the simple dénouement of *just* a casket beneath the earth. Just a headstone to kneel beside.

Where is it that you have gone to? Rainbows overhead? Fallen trees in the backyard? Little shivers of the spine when we sit still long enough to let the memory of you wash over us?

As a kid, you walked by what eventually became the tree that sat in the front yard of the house I once lived in. On the way to dropping me off at elementary school one morning—the same one you attended—you told me that you walked by that oak monster with the outstretched arms when you were my age. I walked and played under that tree 70 years later, which means we walked by one another as boys, The meaninglessness of years and time being the only veil of separation.

There was a raccoon family in that tree when I was a kid. They would look in at me through my bedroom window as I would look at them burrowed in the hollow of a tree branch that had likely been there when you walked by years before. A branch that fell off somewhere along the timeline. As a child, did you ever see the ancestors of these furry friends who would peer in at me late into the evening? Did you witness them when you built the addition on the house all those years later for my parents?

Do we see the ones we love when we see what they love and appreciate those things in the same way? Birds remain fairly proximal. There were likely birds you saw as a boy whose great-great-great grandkids soared over my head as a kid as well.

There is a mystery to all of this that I cannot understand.

The last plane ride you ever took was 2000 miles to and from my new home, to see this place I now occupy. Your eyes and mind — those tools of yours always focused on the wonderful — they saw my dog. They beamed at Emily when she got off work and joined us at Chaps for dinner. They gaped in amazement at the rolling hills and lake surrounding my home—the same ones that I pass by, nearly oblivious.

You have tasted the scone I eat as I write this, raving of its cinnamon flavor. You have seen these birds and hills here, too. Your emotion and your curiosity and your *'youness'* has coalesced in the same spaces I and all that have loved you and that you have loved have focused on.

We share curious points of intersection.

Do we see this?

Like the bugs and the snakes and the birds and the rabbits, the intersections always come back—they always remain. The little patch of planet your rabbit hopped along as you gazed will stay. The trees to which your mind wandered will be in the backyard. The cinnamon scone will retain its flavor.

2000 miles lay between Detroit and Spokane that your eyes have witnessed from out of a plane window —the same miles and land my eyes will witness as I make my way back home to celebrate you. If who we are is a consequence of what we appreciate, these miles are testament to the fact that there is more place and space to marvel and explore and discover little remnants of your appreciation than your whole family could cover in all its collective lifetime.

Because you were one to look out the window.

The finite attaches itself to slivers of the infinite during its time within space and scope. And when the finite leaves us, it extends its arms from the places it looked at and marveled at and attached itself to, inviting us into eternal embrace for the duration of its memory.

We may have lost you, but we can never lose *you*. You extend and whisper from every crevice and space you gazed upon and to which you projected your heart. And for you, that was a constant process. That's the birds and the snakes and the trees. That's the rabbits.

That's all of us.

Are We Seeing This?

There are puzzle pieces that have been littered everywhere throughout the course of your life. They are put together with participation in the same process you partook in so well; a process of unabashed love dedicated to discovering and giving oneself to the reality that... *there is enough mystery in our midst to sustain our curiosity for a lifetime.* A treasure hunt with no chest at the end but little bits and shimmers of you every step along the way.

I will see you there, on that walk with that intent of wonder and curiosity, every day, for the rest of my life. And in doing so, I will pass you along to those I extend myself to as well—those who would never have known you in the flesh. I will stand beside you, gazing. And the reality of your being will never stop returning, like the rabbits to your backyard; like the fireflies on a summer night; like the wonder that glossed over your eyes as you peered in awe.

The Deep Time of Holes

When I was about 5-10 years old, my grandpa, who I
called *Papa,* dug a hole. I can't remember exactly why he
dug this hole, but a hole was dug, and I found myself
down in the hole with him. It was located to the west
of the house. East of the pond. Plopped in the middle
of ten or so acres of land he and my *Nonnie* lived on.

While down in this hole that rose to the top of my
young head, Papa used his right pointer finger to trace
downward diagonally across layers of soil, sand, clay
and rock.

"You're looking at thousands of years right here,"
Papa said. "Each layer is a different era. Different types
of rock exist within each. Can you see? With a good
eye, you can see from the coloring the different
happenings in the era you're looking at."

I watched as his finger traveled centuries, millennia,
not knowing what I was seeing but also knowing,
intuitively, that I was small.

The frogs from the pond nearby carried on with
their steady croaking. The cicadas swirled and sung
above. Robins landed softly to the south on the old
wooden fence with birdseed strewn beneath. The snake

living in the cattails, a Blue Racer, wriggled its way down toward the water.

15-20 years have passed since then. Not enough time to leave its mark in that hole. I sit 2000 miles away. Married and discovering my first gray beard hair. Papa sits at home battling cancer. And what seems like an eternity in the scope of the two of our lives, is nothing.

In the time of the hole, we are still standing there within.

Papa passed about 2 weeks after writing this. I think back to that hole on those 10 acres a lot. And how time folds and holds and connects. And how what we lose both *remains* and *continues* in memory.

A Bridge

In the year 1936
my grandfather walked by a tree on his way to school
When I was 8 years old,
he recalled a decade or so ago.

70 some years later, as a boy of the same age, I saw that
same tree
It was outside my bedroom window
My family moving into the house he walked by
him coming over for BBQs and birthdays
staring upward at the marvel oak
exceeding what his young mind could ever have
imagined

Generations of bird lived there
I saw baby raccoons and their mother living in a hollow
from my window
so many cycles of leaves from his boyhood to mine
collapsing onto the earth
cycling back into the space and time
woven and weaved
Bridging the illusion of years

And now he's gone
and I am no longer a young child
but we are webbed

Are We Seeing This?

Him carrying memory of the tree into his passing
me over miles

Everything is an icon - a bridge - to everything else

Mike Christie

Observations in the Key of a Slow and Gradual Confluence

A man with hair halfway down his back, and a scraggly beard—both powder white—rides by on an old dirt bike. It is sunny, in the upper 60s, between 9 and 10 a.m. It is late May.

There is another man seated on the patio of this coffee shop I'm sitting at, cradling a classical guitar and moving his hand up and down the fretboard. Not fast, but intentionally. Hitting each chord and note with precision and patience.

There were also two ladies who were seated on the navy blue Adirondack chairs who were talking about their kids and their lives and I couldn't help but imagine both wanted the conversation over as soon as possible so they could head home and put on gardening gloves and reach into the soil and sift around a bit and plant what needs to be planted because that's just how they *seemed,* if you know what I mean.

A friend of mine, who also happened to be at this locale, walked up behind me and said hello, telling me about what they are writing and their dating woes and how the last thing they expected became what they encountered when it came to an individual they re-converged with the other day.

And now I'm back alone with focus being buttons and fingers and screen and putting down ideas and observations on this document. I have not been doing this much lately. I don't believe it is imposter syndrome like I've experienced in the past, but I have been avoiding writing for a while. It's merely the feeling that sometimes wells run dry and we need to walk away and then come back, which doesn't seem all that profound, and probably doesn't need to be.

Life bubbles up and beckons in all moments, I think, which is a rather unreasonable thing to say and speak if you haven't been attentive enough to watch it happen. But I am so quick to be critical as it relates to what I truly care about. So quick to water down that which I want to be *dense* and *full-bodied* and I do not know why I do this to myself but I am trying to learn.

For some reason of which I am only vaguely aware — but also for reasons that don't need awareness or meaning but just *are* and that's why they matter — the previously mentioned observations matter to me. Deeply. I sense, when I pause *just* long enough, that there is some great occurrence or song or film or story, all loosely flowing with the same current. And that it's taking us somewhere. And the current and story are narrowing and that eventually — God, I hope this is true — we will meet and meld and learn to love and dance. And we will be compelled to be together and to see one another and to peek beyond the invisible ideologies we hold, and enjoy and grasp more strongly

the visible abundance of beards and dirt bikes, classical
guitars and sunny days, gardening middle-aged women
and friends and coffee.

Beacons and Bonfires

Every fall in Spokane the burn ban lifts. Our dry summers and wildfire-ravaged landscape put the bonfire at bay in the hotter months. But the leaves change and moisture returns and in mid-October, the backyard gatherings can begin again.

I love sitting by the fire. The chilly evening air. The early darkness. The lingering leaves clinging to their branches. Sometimes it will be just Emily and I out back, with Oliver running around chasing squirrels. Sometimes we'll have a friend or two over. Silence mingles with conversation. And within it all is a presence to *this* fire and *these* people and the scope is warm and manageable.

The other night, for the first time in over two years, we went out to a night club to dance. Covid combined with not-so-nightclubby tendencies led to the drought. We were with a different set of friends. No one on the dance floor was masked so we veered off into a little room under the staircase to the side of all the action. The music was loud and the space was crowded and you couldn't hear a single word anyone was saying.

Sitting in the silence the noise made, I thought about our bonfire pit, and how, since the burn ban lifted, it hadn't been used. I thought about the solar-powered lights that dangle over the top. Collecting the energy for their light from exactly where they are. And how they had probably flickered on since we had left the house. I thought about the different type of silence embracing that space — in the backyard of our house seated at the dead-end of our street.

People like to theorize about whether trees that fall in a forest with nothing to hear them make a sound. Does music and yelling and noise in a club with no comprehension to what is being said yield a silence?

There are beacons and there are bonfires.

A friend told me recently about how there used to be numerous communities around the city who would distribute Thanksgiving baskets every year for less-privileged families. Churches and non-profits passing out supplies within their communities. Sometimes going door to door. Sometimes setting hubs in their facilities for neighbors to walk to. The exchange usually associated with a laugh or words or eye contact or smiles or tears.

Now, some committee focused on efficiency, has consolidated the pocketed practice and directed each parcel and piece to a massive, orchestrated affair at the arena in the center of the city. Thousands of people flock there in their cars on Thanksgiving. Long lines file toward assembly lines. People grab their box of food and go.

On the Michigan land that used to be occupied by my family, the frog the lily pad and the tree and the reeds and the dragonfly and the bluegill and the heron and the painted box turtle and the robin and the worm have all been around awhile. A patch of 10 acres made up of water and marsh and field and forest. And over the course of thousands of years, different iterations of these creatures' ancestors have occupied the same plot. Each species has blurred the lines of self in the way all pieces become other pieces. In the way that all pieces are not so much pieces and are more, in deeper time, wholes unseen.

We're all chasing and making meccas when we have a backyard. Sometimes I wonder what it would look like to create community not so heavily framed by ideology but by place. To know the names of more than just two neighbors. To learn the plants and birds. To learn to distinguish and identify the squirrels that Oliver chases. To give them each a name. To teach Oliver their names.

To only get coffee from the shop on my street. To buy beer only in my neighborhood, and groceries only at the non-existent market in the burrow, and books at the house-turned-bookstore beside the brewery.

We have created beacons we flock to based on interest and ideology, which, of course, is not all bad. We have created havens for those left on the margins via bias and bigotry—the characteristics of our species that may be our undoing. Is there a way to shimmy back into place, though? Into habitat and ecosystem and maybe not always fully receive exactly what the individual mind needs but, instead, melt a little? Make way for some form of mutualism that sheds away a bit of the obsession with the self and its need to be catered to? I am asking myself.

The individual is not an actual fact but a category that depends on one's point of view, says Merlin Sheldrake, the mycologist. In my backyard, the soil is teeming with highways. Fungal mycelium shooting across the landscape blurring the lines of what is what. Above the ground, each on their different seats, friends sit in silence and start melting inward toward the fire. Captivated by its bounding flame. Breathing the same smells. Sharing the same air. Illuminated by the same light.

Knock Knock Knock

I am in the hammock looking upward.
A woodpecker lands on the tree supporting my
suspended bed
and it does what woodpeckers do
Knocking its head against bark above
Ascending bit by bit
After each series of three hammer-headed attempts.

The tree carries the beak-banging action downward.
Each knock
Yields a vibration
that funnels from limb to branch to trunk to hammock
Softly buzzing through its descent
Arriving at me

I am feeling *this*
I am an extension of *this*

This being the knock of a bird beak 25 feet above
This being what the wood conduit of the tree carries
This being hundreds of thousands of years of
biological evolution
and growth
and intention
and development
and choice

This being the habitual pattern of another creature
This being what was happening with or without me
here

knock knock knock

Once more action is shared
Once more the woodpecker's choice arrives within me
through the weird way that vibration is external and
also not

In the weird way that all of this is external and also not.

knock knock knock

I am what the woodpecker is doing

knock knock knock

Perhaps I am what all this is doing?

There is no great distinction
that confluence cannot question and find resolve
through those moments
that we remember
to step beyond

The Mushrooms in the Basement

When he was around the age of 7 or 8, my little brother, Colin, got hooked on mushrooms. A friend introduced him to them, and he fell into the rabbit hole. No, not the psychedelic kind or the idea of pairing them with steaks. At least not exclusively. His obsession was with their classification. His friend had an Audubon guide for mushrooms and my brother's life wouldn't be complete until he had his own copy.

Prior to this, mushrooms had made their presence known around the Christie household. Behind the garage at the house we lived in while I was in grade school, there had been the strangest orange, foamy-textured straw-shaped mushrooms with what looked like green sludge coating their tip. All us siblings would take shovels and slice them in half, retreating to the house due to the pungent smell they produced.

Upon getting his own copy of the guide, Colin and I went to the woods a few times to attempt to classify different fungi we came across. When golfing, he, Jack and I would see different varieties on the course. We'd do our best to remember what they looked like. Sifting through the pages of his book when we got back home, we were hoping to determine whether or not they would have been good on a salad, given us some whacky "wide-awake" type dreams, or just flat out killed us.

The mushroom craze became a bit of a brotherly bond.

Like most odd obsessions that grow from the fertile soil of youth, this one faded over time. The guide has been through two moves and sits, dusty, in the back of Colin's closet. However, after years of silence, they have surfaced again.

The other day I got a photo from Colin. He was down in the laundry room — the unfinished part of my parents' basement — when he came across an old and familiar friend.

A multitude of mushrooms had sprung up from the floor surrounding the drain in the middle of the room; their resiliency and tenacity on full display as they seemed to rise almost inexplicably from concrete. My curiosity was piqued all the more when I imagined the possibility that they crawled up from the depths of the drain. How could life manifest itself from such nothingness? Sure, I've read that bacteria occupy any and every surface on the planet—even the old nuclear reactors of the Chernobyl disaster site. But this was a tangible, living reality that my brother's sense of sight needed no microscopic instrument to observe. It was 'shroom from concrete. And it brought us back.

Are We Seeing This?

I downloaded an app for $5 that advertised the ability to tell you what kind of mushroom you were looking at simply by taking its photo … tech had leapfrogged Audubon. The reviews were good. I had to know what this mushroom was, and I passed on that sense of urgency to Colin.

App downloaded, picture uploaded, no results found. The app couldn't tell me what Colin's curiosity had uncovered. I let him know and he became enamored of the possibility that he had discovered an entirely new species. And even though we both knew that was likely not the case, I sense there's a lesson to be learned in the obsession that surrounded this basement discovery.

I've been occupied a lot lately with the all-too-soul-sucking *busy*. Task after task. Many of which are life giving, some definitely not. And it's in the *next next next* mentality of this task-based life that life has given me the chance to witness and acknowledge the potent, life-affirming trifecta that has been neglected in the back corners of my mind. All from the muse of a mushroom. And that trifecta is…

Wonder, awe and an appreciation for the unlikely.

I've been thinking all day about those mushrooms. How they may have slithered up the drain. And my mind wanders to places of wonder I haven't ventured to in years. *What else could be down there? Portals to different worlds? Magical creatures and beings? Is this really a new species?*

These thoughts are obviously not rational, but that's part of the beauty tied to them! These thoughts are the thoughts I couldn't help but let my mind entertain in my youth. But up until this little mushroom encounter, they had fallen to the wayside. Now having encountered them again, and simply aligning with the joy that comes in that type of wonder, there seems to be... *more*. More vibrancy. More opportunity for the unexpected.

When do we chose not to just as readily entertain these realities? When along our journey do we chose to move from joy in the unlikely to accomplishment in the mundane? The satisfaction of accomplishment is immediate, and the cycle keeps going — there's always something more to do. But leaning into the story of the unlikely takes time. Takes a mind that's open. In our obsession with accomplishment, the unlikely doesn't often carry much weight. And as we become more inclined toward accomplishment than creation, it makes sense the former takes precedent. But maybe that whole context of emphasis is skewed.

I believe it's in the places of imagined worlds tied to the mushrooms, tied to the wonder of the everyday, that we discover there's *infinite possibility*.

I have a friend who upon graduating college had a really hard time with the idea of being human. He saw himself as a hinderance to the natural way of the world. More than anything, he saw himself and humanity as hindering the ability of all other life to exist as it should.

So, one day, fitting with the theme of the rest of this, he found a particular type of mushroom and popped it in his mouth. And he immediately lost all sense of creativity or wonder or awe or whatever you want to call it. He simply and only felt the reality of survival. Whether that was finding the next task to accomplish, the next meal, place to sleep, you name it. Via his consumption of this mushroom, his experience with reality was on tasks and tasks alone. And when he came back to his sober state, he realized what he believed to be the beauty of being human that he had missed before — *we have a chance to imagine and create and discover.* To open our minds to more than simply the task in front of us.

I believe my friend's story reveals something that is important, even if difficult for us to accept.

In our advanced and civilized state, in this *go go go* world we occupy, we've placed so much emphasis on the task that we've lost a critical piece of our humanity. We've lost touch with our imagination. Our ability to wonder and be curious and think of the story behind the story.

I want to wonder about the mushrooms in the basement. I want to give myself to the stories my mind paints about worlds that arise from deep within the drain. I want to imagine, even if I don't truly believe, that the species my brother found is new and has never before been discovered. Not because I want to be careless and ill-informed, not because I want to neglect the need for rationality, not because I want to not get done what needs to be done...

But because I want to always leave room for the possible rather than just the prescribed when I interact with the world in front of me.

The Way of Wind and Water

Beneath Spokane, there is a large reservoir containing
water for city use. A kindergartner is using
some right now as he sips from the fountain outside his
class. Above Spokane are clouds containing water that
will soon be falling on the residents below, one in
particular named Ronald.   He is meandering through
the streets when, suddenly, his vision is obstructed by a
drop hitting his glasses. To Spokane's south reside the
rolling hills of the Palouse. On the grass of the Palouse
sit tiny specks of water droplets from an automatic
sprinkler that seems to have forgotten that it's January
and that it's cold and that all that needs watering is fast
asleep. To the east of Spokane are the large lakes of the
Idaho panhandle, Coeur d'Alene and Pend Oreille. On
the northeast corner of lake Coeur d' Alene, a few
ducks paddle along in search of a mid-afternoon snack.
To the north of Spokane sit the Selkirk's, snowy rolling
peaks where skiers shoot down runs. A skier named
Kevin picks up snow from the higher elevations, kicks
off his skis and walks back to his car. The snow melts
and wets the roof of his Rav4 as he drives back home.
The water trickles down his windshield and he turns on

the wipers. To the west of Spokane flows the mighty Columbia, which a hundred rivers and creeks empty into. One such tributary sees a trout tumble into the much larger body of water. Disoriented, the trout gives into the river's might. A river that ultimately empties itself into the largest body of water of them all, the Pacific. Flowing through Spokane is the Spokane river. This came from lake Coeur d'Alene to the east and will flow to the Columbia to the west. A trout or two may tumble from it as well. Disoriented but *with* and *in* and *within* the flow.

Beneath Spokane, the roots of an oak at Manito Park that formed from seeds that littered
themselves into place thanks to wind that blew through the area 84 years ago. Above Spokane, an airplane is bouncing about and some flyer is wiping sweaty palms on jeans because the wind isn't wanting to be nice to the anxieties of this troubled passenger as the flight descends. To the south of Spokane, over those same Palouse hills, there are few trees, so wind picks up steam and knocks the hat off a chick pea farmer walking out to his car to head to the grocery store because his wife is out of sugar and wants to make cookies and he'll do *anything* for a cookie. To the east of Spokane, wind knocks over a ponderosa pine that had been dead for some time but finally gave way between the heaviness of the snow and the breeze pushing through. A squirrel had just hopped from the branch of the tree and looks back as it collapses to the earth

and doesn't understand the event but also feels quite powerful all of a sudden. To the north of Spokane, a person steps outside without her coat zipped up, the wind whooshes into her open coat and she is immediately overcome with a chill and says '*fuck*' accidentally and her seven-year-old looks up at them, eyes expanding, and says '*oooooohhh.*' To the west of Spokane, in the barrenness of central Washington, one of the many tumbleweeds occupying the landscape scurries out onto I-90 and goes underneath a 2005 white Chevy Malibu and makes the subtlest of noises as it's caught under the car and will continue to do so. The driver has finally had enough and pulls off at the Moses Lake exit with the Starbucks and orders a mocha, only to forget why he had stopped, and gets back onto I-90 only to hear the tumbleweed again. Through Spokane, the wind knocks a cubed garden plot off a second story balcony which then falls into an alley in front of an Australian shepherd and its owner. They both look at each other and the owner gives the Aussie a treat for its near peril and awards himself one too, but the human kind. A scone.

In Israel, about 2000 years ago, Jesus told some priest that the way of the Divine is best seen in the way of wind and water.

The priest didn't understand.

The Dragonfly Mecca

In the springtime
my dead-end dirt road becomes a sort of Mecca
for dragonflies.
Evenings in May are clouded with their swirling
the patch of road between my house and the one a
door to the west
like Sturgis in summer.
Four-winged miracles blister the air and dance with one
another.

Who am I to say that this is not holy ground for
another species?
That my mark of earth
is not their Giza or Sistine?
There are so many species
so many places
could not every piece be the great place of
convergence
for a kind?

It's fall now
and the days are shorter and cooler.
We are returning from a walk
On which we talked about the organized spiritual being
not of much weight or importance any longer.
The dog in tow

Are We Seeing This?

looking back with every mention of his name
grinning
and as we head down our dead-end dirt lane
a single spec.
Four-winged buzzing
carving out its path in front of us
approaching the end of the street and soaring upward
a lone dragonfly.
No more great bumble of communion
but a solitary soaring
reaching the end
traveling upward and
beyond and
disappearing.

Remembering Ron

When you become a pastor, you don't know who you'll meet. When you move a church, you don't know who will show up. I became a pastor at a church that had recently moved. I was starting fresh. *We* were starting fresh. A new occupation, a new locale, and an empty slate to see what would become and unfurl.

When Branches moved to West Central, we didn't really know what to expect. We were largely a group of individuals migrating from a northside setting to one downtown; and packaged into that move were all the metaphors you can pull out of such locale distinctions. The upper middle-class descending upon the working-class community. The undertones of gentrification.

We had lots of raised eyebrows watching us from outside during that season. And rightfully so! We were naive and willing to learn and naive all the same.

The first few Sundays in the new building were packed with northside transplants shooting south for the service. But over time, old faces steadily left, and new ones showed up. And one of the first new additions to our updated address was a tall, lanky, older man with the kindest face I think I've ever seen.

Squat of flex and strength.
Eyes brilliant and bright.
Presence soft and serene.
Laugh of deep-bellied breath.
Early into our move, Branches met Ron.

Ron was an older gentleman with an intellectual
disability who lived in a care facility down the street.
Ron enjoyed 8 creamers and 10 sugars in his coffee.
Ron enjoyed a cigarette out front of the building
during worship with Marvin, the scent of which
became Branches' unofficial incense. Ron enjoyed
laughing when laughter seemed an odd response. Ron
loved Mountain Dew... at 10 a.m. Ron beamed and
giggled at kids who would then giggle and beam back at
him. Ron was gentle. Ron gave the best hugs. Ron, a
year or so in, remembered my name. Ron took
communion with attentive anticipation. During one
such communion, Ron, while looking at me and
squatting, eyes shimmering; me, looking at him while
squatting, eyes shimmering... spoke to me softly in his
raspy and grizzled voice,

"Mike — you're a good pastor. Good pastor, Mike.
Yeah."

He said this to me during a season where most days
I would beat myself up inside unendingly throughout
the week — saying the complete opposite about myself.
Living in that weird, internal, often unspoken space
seemingly all pastors live but don't really know how to

articulate or admit but that pervades and pummels and persists within. Imposter syndrome, denial, *why am I doing this*, etc.

I've written a lot about Ron, and mentioned him in many a sermon. He was the embodiment of what I—and I sense many at Branches—found compelling about the rhythm of a Sunday morning service. He was the representation of what kept all of us attending this thing that many of our peers saw as outdated or dangerous or unnecessary.

We didn't show up for *just* the theology or songs or sermons. Anyone at Branches had been burned or burnt out enough by such things for them to be the main draw.

What brought us back was the reality that every Sunday morning at 10:00 there was a routine that Ron and Alan and Ali and Andrew and Adi and Mackenzie and Meghan and Mark and Marvin and all these people of varied backgrounds and contexts and stories shared and intersected and converged within. 1804 W. Broadway was a confluence for distinct worlds.

The reality of *that* floored me. It inspired me.

But then COVID happened, and that inspiring and flooring piece has been put on pause. I haven't seen Ron in months because his facility has been on lockdown. But today I found myself at Ron's care home for duties tied to another job I had gotten due to COVID slowing down pastoral things. And I mentioned to an employee who worked there that I knew Ron and I said so with a joy and appreciation and pep that naturally popped out of me at the thought of the man.

And that's when it happened... The employee's smile remained, but it became a somber smile. I think we all can picture that kind of smile. A smile traced with love and affection for a memory. But for a *memory*, not for a *present*.

"Ah. Ron actually passed away a couple weeks ago."

Suddenly, all the memory of that pre-covid *happening* that was Branches — all the lives and stories of all varieties and the weird and wacky community that gathered and made up and intersected in the building a couple blocks over — that memory punched me in the gut.

Suddenly, Ron's smile and his trembling, sugar-coated hands — his misty eyes and guttural laugh — it all came flooding in.

Suddenly, all that we have missed but have become numb to missing, hit and shattered and tossed me.

I was flooded with sadness. I won't hear that laugh again. I won't look into those eyes again. I won't see that smile again.

I was flooded with guilt. That my only intersections were through the Sunday morning context. That I hadn't kept in touch. That I hadn't reached out.

But I was also flooded with appreciation.

People flow and they push past the parameters we place on them. We don't really lose what we lose. Every week, Ron would ask me for a Bible. He is, if I'm being honest, the only person at Branches during my tenure to make that request — ha! That's just who we are. And each week I'd give him New Testaments stored in the building, and my wife Emily and I gave him a large-text Bible for Christmas one year. But inevitably, every week he'd come back and ask for another. Eventually, out of curiosity and because it was the other church's Bibles who we shared the space with that I kept handing out… I had to ask what was wrong with each of the ones I had given him in the past. His response was simple and pointed:

"I finished it."

I have no idea what spirituality is "about." But I know for certain it is not "about" the assumptions and parameters we place on it. I am a pastor (and so are you) and I don't know what I believe. A good chunk of the time I don't know if I believe that there is *a God* or not.

I don't know if the story about *hopeful possibility* I am telling myself and my congregants is real or something I simply tell myself to make meaning.

I don't know if I am helping or hurting more.

I don't know if my pursuits are worth the energy and the time and the frustration and the confusion and the heartache associated with them.

I *hope* for such things. But I don't *know* them.

And I certainly think the same can be said about the reality of the church and whatever nebulous meaning that word entails. But I do know that Ron came back every Sunday. That he was drawn to the love of the people of Branches. And that the people of Branches were drawn to the love of Ron and one another. And whatever that is — that mystery and presence and flow that draws uniquely different worlds toward one another — I believe in that.

Mike Christie

These Places Still Exist

Sometimes I think of silent situations and sanctuaries.
This time, my imagination takes me to a small town in
northern Michigan. No particular town. But a simple,
tiny spot nestled on a lake next to a larger lake. And
when I go there, I'm reminded of a family who has just
adopted twins. The couple is on the older side—late
40s—for embarking on the journey of parenthood.
They tried for years to have their own, but with no
success. They live a quiet life in a relatively quiet town.
She's a doctor, he's an artist. And their children are
lovely and fun and bubbly and the way in which they all
exist is like the way the oak in their front yard exists
after 84 years even though these babies have only
existed for 84 weeks and even though it is hard to even
qualify what that might mean.

The family is still and calm and silent and it's early
evening. There's orange in the sky … and purple and
pink and blue and white and colors we don't know the
names of. The husband and the wife sit on the porch
out front and rock on their porch swing and the babies
are on the other side of an open window, asleep in
separate cribs. And the parents sip on cherry wine, this

being the one week a year they allow themselves to indulge in the touristy beverage that fills every boutique on the main road in town, just down the hill from their house.

The babies don't burble or bumble a peep. And the man and the woman don't say anything at all to one another. She rests her head on his shoulder, and as the sun is about to slink away until the following day, the last of it illuminates the pastoral scene. Yes, the weening light, the little bit of light that's the smallest the light has been since its mirrored counterpart earlier this morning; it illuminates it all. The lake and the neighbors' homes and the town below and the boats on the lake and the toes of the babies inside that are *just* peeking out of their baby blankets and the softest kiss in the world the husband plants on his wife's forehead and the subtle cherry wine mustache above the wine drinker's upper lip.

Inhaling the Lost

I am inhaling the lost
ashes to ashes
dust to dust
towering trees
homes
loved things
flesh
lie to rest in my lungs.

Form to formlessness
has found form again.
That which existed and ceased
now passes in and through
baptizing in its loss.
Former flame inflaming.

Even as fires engulf
we are not separate but built from one another.
Only this time ash
no holy water to be had.

Destruction and integration
yield separateness, unified.

What will have final say
as we all seep into final form?

Are We Seeing This?

Tenhave

On certain occasions at dusk while I was in high school, a buddy and I would drive to a set-aside patch of forest in our hometown the size of a city block. We'd write our name and the date on golf balls, tee them up in an open field beside the woods, swing the driver back, swing through, and head into the wildness with headlamps in search of what we had just ridded ourselves of.

This happened during summer in Michigan. And although the sunlight may let up after a certain point, the Michigan humidity lays stagnant and punctuated in the thick evening air of July.

We'd wade through fallen trees and fallen leaves and thickets of still upright trees and we'd march through marshy soil. We'd swat at mosquitos and lurch at the sound of cicadas and trip on tree roots.

Occasionally we'd stumble past temporary encampments of the local campers. They always appeared unoccupied but the slight rustling that we both knew came from neither of our movements made us think the one who did occupy was not too far off.

I'm not sure if we ever found one of the golf balls we hit. The combination of dense, deciduous forest and muddy, leafy ground hid them well.

It's funny how the initial pursuit of retrieval can ultimately yield contentment with the search.

I don't know how many times I've found what I was pursuing. Each time I arrive, that thing, whatever it was, grows and evolves and moves beyond what was initially sought. But in the rummaging and the searching is the memory made. Of time in the woods. Of meaning manifesting. Not finding the golf ball is to continue to operate in the mystery of knowing it's out there, somewhere, but not tracked down. Not contained. Still elusive and mysterious.

Which is perhaps the recipe for all good things.

Which is certainly the recipe for wonder.

The Froggy Father

A man told me his dad was 'froggy' the other day. I had not heard the term. He was wearing a Dead and Co T-shirt that he admitted was not a byproduct of his own attendance to a show of the Grateful Dead's latest iteration but was a gift from a friend. He was a self-proclaimed *Dead Head* though. One of the crustier old hippies that, it became clear over a ten-minute interaction full of complaint and bitterness, turned flowers and free love into resentment and disdain as he aged.

Bummer.

But his dad was *froggy*. Which, I found out later after a quick Google search, meant *jumpy or flighty*. Characteristics that frogs do indeed seem to possess!

Right on.

Froggy has since become a favorite term of mine. However, even though said in an endearing Nor-Cal hippy drawl that I aspire to on certain days, the old hippy spoke of his father's *froginess* with a tinge of remorse.

Twelve kids. Always gone. Remarried to a woman only three years older than his son who had told me all

59

this. The memory of the froggy father didn't leave much room for levity and ease.

Did this man with the froggy father run off to find paternal peace in the likes of Jerry Garcia and his Dead Head posse? Dancing and acid taking and flower weaving, helping simmer down a boiling boy who never knew his dad? And, after years of following the band and dancing in the rain and meeting many to love a little but no one to love a lot, did he, slowly sure, but still, all the same... become... froggy himself?

It seems to me that when the head is down, we run down many different paths that tend to converge in the place the path initially set out to avoid.

Here We Are

This morning my eyes opened
they saw the room the wife the carpet
they began again.
This does not stop until it does
and then does not.
Do we think about this enough?

Are we here when here we are?

All I have seen
has died or has not
no departure, regardless
Only tripping into time
laid to rest awhile
to return again
with eyes wide open.

Every space of this earth is a bed
to wake and to rest
for the eyes to see
to begin again.

Mike Christie

Are We Seeing This?

My wife and I woke up early and took a walk. Not *early* early. There were, after all, three hits of the snooze button prior to embarking. But early enough that the sun was hovering low still, as were most people. So, we found ourselves more or less alone. Except for one lone car that swooped in front of us with a woman behind the wheel; she wore the face of stress and of being somewhere else. We paused. She passed, and we carried on.

It's late March. The weather seems to be turning. Back and forth bickering between winter's cold and spring's chill present in the air. Patches of blue seeable amidst an otherwise cloud-clustered sky. Rain falling and being made known through the wind. The wind pushing it diagonally in such a way that it *hit* our face rather than grazed it in the way that rain, delicate when left to its own devices, would have preferred to greet our skin.

Not many words were exchanged. Our bodies transitioning from sleep to consciousness, like the world around. Little bulbs of flowers I don't know the names of had begun to unwrap the dirt-sheets covering their bedded-bodies in their slow and steady unfurling, making their way up and out.

We brought the dog along. His unfurling accelerated far more quickly than any flower or human brain not having yet met its coffee counterpart that day. He sniffed his way around. Tracing life that had passed these parts prior, and investigating the life present.

At one point, a squirrel slipped in along the path we were taking. Bold, sure. But I'm convinced at this point in my dog-walking life that squirrels are aware of leashes and see them as their great partner in the game of torment they like to play with our barking, whining, furry friends. This particular squirrel appeared about 20 yards in front of us on the sidewalk. It looked back to see us approaching, bounded along, and then jumped off the pavement to the right onto a thin and narrow branch of a bare bush, eventually using the branch to climb up to the first accessible tree limb.

There was nothing all that extraordinary about the interaction. I don't think anyone but me even noticed. Oliver the dog did his usual flailing of the body, subtle whining, accelerated trotting. But again, nothing particularly out of character.

As our feet made their way to where the squirrels' feet had been moments earlier, the branch it had hopped onto was still bouncing up and down.

I never took a physics class, which is a sore spot between my siblings and I who slogged through theirs. But in seeing this bouncing branch from the squirrel, my limited understanding went to Newton and his laws of motion. The branch was stagnant, the squirrel was not. And by the squirrel hopping onto the dormant branch, the branch became dormant no more.

I'm not going to spend too much time in the weeds explaining what expertise I lack, but I do have wonder. And as we walked past the still bouncing branch, my mind couldn't help but think of all the other pieces associated with its bouncing. For example:

Like how I had hit the snooze button three times that morning.

Like how that woman in the car was coming from wherever she was coming from at the same moment we were coming from where we were coming from and how we had to wait for her to drive past to cross the street.

Like how our dog had to pee *and* poop, two pit stops, which delayed our arrival to this moment in space and time.

Like how my wife walks at about 3.6 miles per hour and I walk at about 2.9 miles per hour and how we have to meet in the middle at around 3.3 miles per hour when we walk together.

Like how some combination of weather patterns in the North Cascades and perhaps even further west in the Northern Pacific led to rain arriving *this* morning on *this* day. The rain doing what it did, in ways evident but not known, to affect timing and intersection.

Like how the squirrel may have been doing whatever the hell squirrels are doing early in the morning and got distracted or inspired and arrived on the scene just then.

Like how that branch came from some bush that was planted or that a bird dropped the seeds to however many years ago and the sun and rain and weather of the last however many years caused it to grow and expand and become and create a branch that hovered *just* in the way and place that that branch hovered.

And how all that led to the branch still bouncing as I walked past it even though the squirrel was gone and the dog had calmed and the rain still fell.

I have *this* job rather than *that* job because of interactions like these. I love *this* person rather than *that* person because of interactions like these. I am a son and brother and husband and enemy and friend rather than organic matter in some other form somewhere else… because of interactions like these.

People spend so much time and write exegesis and create careers and introduce ideologies built around answering the question as to *where* the interaction comes from. What the source behind the *why* of all this is. But we are here and here is now and now is a piece and part of the history of all that ever was. And all that ever will be is formed from all that is happening here because of all that has happened. And sources may not matter.

Are we seeing this?

Mike Christie

Horsies

When we were kids, my sister would stare out the window as my family drove from Metro Detroit to the Florida Panhandle, accelerated seasonal change zooming past as we shot down I-75. Gradual greening of the grass. Buds blooming and becoming. Sweeping away the gray of our northern peninsula.

"HORSIES," she would yell as we drove past a cow pasture.

"No Catherine. Those are cows," my jaded 10-year-old self would reply. Refusing to let slide a bovine being misperceived as a stallion.

But then we'd pass another field and she would think she was seeing horses again and it didn't do me or anyone else any good to continue correcting her. So, we drove by "horse" farms and shifting seasons and, eventually, arrived at the beach.

A friend told me recently that children see the world and their reality as if it were illuminated by a lantern. And that, as we get older, the lantern gradually becomes more of a spotlight, rationality replacing holistic curiosity. Gradually, we move away from the

idea of our perception being equally interesting.
Gradually, we move away from not needing to dissect
in order to discover. Gradually, we move away from
being fully *here.*

Another friend sent me this Virginia Woolfe quote
recently:

*I will cut adrift—I will sit on pavements and drink coffee—I
will dream; I will take my mind out of its iron cage and let it
swim—this fine October.*

Imagine an aquarium at the bottom of the ocean. It
is, of course, full of water. It may have some kelp.
Some ornate rocks. And within it there's a fish,
swimming around the periphery of its glass-walled
world. Amazed by what it has within it. But the glass
walls reflect. They mirror back to the fish its little place
at the bottom of the sea. But just beyond is even more
of this. More vast. Not self-contained. It goes on
forever, seemingly. It is varied and diverse.

The Hubble space telescope took a photo with a
million second exposure back in 2003. It homed in on a
tiny little fraction of the night sky. And it gave us The
Hubble Ultra Deep field photograph— tiny little
galaxies like grains of sand. Millions of stars within
each. Millions of little earths within each. The
seemingly infinite multiple galaxies and worlds—at least
in the context of anything we can fathom—contained
in 3-5 pixels.

The average sidewalk square is 2'x4'. Every spoonful
of dirt contains over a billion life forms. There's a lot

of ways to stutter wonder. But there's also a lot of space to swim.

What are the notes between musical notes? What does it sound like the moment a leaf breaks off a branch? What aroma is emitted from a dragonfly's back when its wings begin to flutter? Where does a joke go when it doesn't land?

A mouse made its way out of the field. On a patch of dirt drive, it looked up to the house on the horizon. Warmth and shelter. Snow was coming. Its young were coming. This was the place and this made sense. And so it scurried along and found an opening. Slipping and slithering and nesting in the basement nook and cranny. And life arrived and the mouse was tender tending to it.

An Interaction Today in Praise of the United States Postal Service

There was a new mailman today. He was short and kind and old and looked a lot like Anthony Fauci. His glasses were rounded and his face was weathered but not beaten, and as he neared my house he said, *hey there* in the most silent and gentle of ways that it caused me not to jolt from the land of Harry Potter (which I was reading on the front porch) but transition from it in a way that led to presence and tenderness washing over the landscape of the interaction.

Do you know what I mean when I describe what this was? When time and space and people and place and who we are and who another is and what the wind is doing and how the cars sound and the soaring of bird songs — *all of it* — inexplicably resolve and land and bloom into nothing more and nothing less than what is? And that *is*-ness could not be a greater gift?

You have a great day now, he said upon handing off two pieces of junk mail. He walked across the street, the old man with letters and bills and publications and Amazon parcels slung across his side. Jovial and jolly.

There are many things to be grateful for and many
things to become disenchanted by. But every
day except Sunday (and sometimes, mysteriously, *also*
Sunday) someone carrying all sorts of story and
message pops up onto your porch. And if you happen
to be sitting there at just the right time, you intersect
with that great wizard.

There is nothing more human than another human.
Junk mail, parcel or package, whatever they pass along,
their presence is a story as rich as the words of the
inevitable heartfelt letter that sits somewhere in their
stash, entrusted to them to pass along.

Tumble

Do you remember?
Seated silently and alone
you waited for the heater to turn on
to warm you and the words of the worlds you whirled
within.
Was there rest there?

Years tumble toward cycle
vexed, you're everywhere you begin.

Journey not too far
back to another moment
of hope and continue
or retreat and retract

Or maybe it is all both?

I wanted to smell the leaves decompose this year
but I got busy.

I wanted to write another book
but I didn't.

In the reading and in the tizzy
has been everything
and I am grown from it

and I am from it
and I am it.

And I will continue
in what I continue.

The Spaces that Hold Us

New house, new neighborhood, new turning of the season; new walks.

There is a street that rounds like a T-shirt collar. It looks out over east Spokane in a panorama. Highway and concrete in the foreground. Mountains and cloud beyond. Ponderosa everywhere. The dog and I have made it a routine to come here after the 10-hour work day.

I am melting with every step. Attempting to allow myself to exhale out the immense weight of the stories working in supportive housing presents you with. Inhaling the vastness of the world outside the walls of occupation.

We reach the edge of the road where moss and grass-covered rock ascend slightly. This is where we sit. And Oliver's haulty comes off his nose. And I pet him and pat him and hold him.

My counselor and I talked about what it means to be held awhile back. And how so much stimuli shoots in and out of us it can be hard to feel centered. When he mentioned this, I thought of Oliver. I've joked that he doesn't know where his body ends and the world begins. Every time I hold him he eases the tense shake and wiggle he often can't keep from expressing. And when I hold him, I also come back to myself, too. I gather the scattered pieces that have escaped and return home to my body, as best I can.

The view is shimmering. The mandarin-orange sky makes creative even concrete. The mountains are shadowed mounds. The city and the beyond bleed in color cast.

Breathe, breathe, breathe.

I imagine this same place before. Rolling hill and river *still* running through. Mountains *still* playing parameter. I imagine me before. Body *still* playing parameter.

Landscape, the personal and the place, may grow and shift, but border is there to contain the random firing received and released. There are millions of words that are floating invisible over the city. Love and last, first and fright. We cannot see them. But they are there. In the caverns of the cars driving by. Many would rise above the highway if they were to become visible. Few and far between out in the hills. Add on emotion and feeling to the invisible becoming visible... if it and words were to float like fog, I would see nothing of the place. All would be cloaked. The physical holds what is not physical.

I wonder about returning to the physical. Of remembering all that the city and the land it is seated upon hold. It groans from the weight of our presence and influence. But it keeps hosting. Offering us endless chances to partner. Its body longs to be tended to as it carries our invisibility.

I wonder about remembering all that the body holds. Emotion creeks invisibly inward and fills with fog.

Return to your feet, bare and brave. Let them return to the earth, soil and subtle. There is an intersection here — a mutual holding. A mutual reminder; a knocking on the door. And an entering for the two into the house of the other. A return home.

We begin the walk again.

Someone at the Stoplight

Inevitably, someone who you turned and looked at…
while sitting at a stoplight… at some point in your
life… is now dead.

I don't know how many people we look at while
stuck in traffic throughout our lives. Probably
thousands. Maybe millions? But someone at whom you
stared during stoplight stopping… they are gone.

And when they left, there were tears shed and
heartbreak happenings and people shared their memories
of love and life and remembered the now deceased
stoplight individual as a child, and up until the day they
departed and everything between.

Maybe, as a kid, they loved to make blueberry
muffins with their mom. And every time they smelled
blueberry muffins they thought of her. And after she
died, they teared up about 47% of the time they walked
into a bakery. Maybe.

Maybe, as a kid, they helped their dad find a wrench
one day and when they found it, their dad smiled at
them—like *really* smiled. A true and real look of pride.
And in that moment, they knew that their dad loved
them and they went back to that memory weekly

throughout the duration of their life. Not because they
had to work for their dad's love but because their dad's
dad was gone before they could say the world "dad" so
the way their dad loved was subtle, even while
overflowing in his heart.

Maybe, when you saw them at the stoplight, they
were on their way to visit that mom or dad or both. At
a gravesite. And what you couldn't see were the flowers
on the passenger seat. Baby's Breath.

Or maybe it wasn't quite so poetic.

Maybe they were on their way to Arby's for lunch
and remembered the smile from their dad and their
mom's laughter and they smiled at the drive-thru
worker and made that worker *laugh* by telling a joke that
had to do with a ladybug.

Someone you saw stopped at a stoplight is dead
now and there's no way we can quantify what their life
was or wasn't. But I think about this sometimes and I
think about how we are flowing in this sea of story that
wishes and wonders and whispers and worships every
little piece of the honey-thick, honey-sweet life in
which we are all somehow dance partners, and I never
want to miss the fact that even the passive moments are
sacred displays of fireworks.

Intersections Among Us

In my line of work as a case manager, there is a fairly clear distinction between client and provider.
Such distinction is important. It helps create a dynamic of objective assistance. My clients know that I fulfill a role and that they can depend on me to fulfill the assigned categories of my position.

But this isn't always easy for me. I'm about the confluence and convergence and connection. For me, where humans intersect with one another is the good stuff. It's gleaming. It's brimming with possibility, vitality and curiosity.

So when I started working in this position, I thought creatively about what could be the intersection point; the place where role — or perhaps more pointedly, the masks—of client and provider could be placed on the back burner. Even if only for a moment. What space could I create where the human — the one who had experienced homelessness and the one who came from a privileged middle-class background — could simply be people together?

Queue The Book of Frogs—the dense, hardcover book that sits on the shelf above my desk; a book that every day my clients and I browse when on hold with some agency with painful hold music; the book clients seek out when they are bored; the book that has led to favorite frogs being picked and written down on frog cutouts now littering my glass office door.

Nearly everyone has seen a frog. And when we see one, we stop what we are doing and we look at those green or orange or purple or red or seemingly *any color* critter.

Frogs are an intersection.

I was speaking with a friend today. And we were riffing about the tendency to home in on distinction rather than connection, and how it divorces us from confluence, harmony and understanding. Nearly everyone has seen a frog. Nearly everyone has seen children play, with joy in their eyes. Nearly everyone has witnessed spring time.

There are intersections littered among us, and within them, there is the possibility of human encountering human, being encountering being. The possibility of seeing that the stranger is not all that strange, but is, rather, a witness to the world and its wonder, just as we are.

We are not that far away from one another. Many streams feed the same river. And their trajectory is *toward*. May we flow the same ... distinctly ... together.

Mike Christie

Bloom

My coworker and I were deep in the abyss of filing paperwork when we hit a roadblock. We were having trouble finding the answer to one of the questions in the *permanent supportive housing* lease paperwork we were navigating. The document asked our agency to provide the *first date of contact* with the individual with whom we were working—individuals who were formerly experiencing homelessness and who are now housed in the *haven* apartment that we work in.

Upon reading this *first date of contact* request, it occurred to me that our universe is rather large. And within such *largeness* is an abundance of mystery. And one such mystery is the possibility of life beyond the realm of our planet, Earth. So, amidst all this, it struck me that — at the same moment we were digging through files trying to discover this answer of *first date of contact* — somewhere, across the universe, there could very well be some stressed-out alien lifeforms digging through their version of files trying to answer the *same* question about some human they had recently abducted.

Are We Seeing This?

I know the location was Roswell, but what was the date we actually made contact with Wendy Bones?

I dwelled in this satisfied state of inquirial convergence for a while.

Much of daily rhythm and routine seems laced with a juice that is rarely drunk. What is it with monotony that subdues inquiry? Points of questioning — which are one whimsy away from wonder — are strewn around us, seemingly at all times! But to take shovel to soil and unearth what that *might be* at any given moment is at best forgotten and, at worst, scolded.

How far back does our memory go? Do we think far enough behind to remember that there was a point where what we are doing and how we are spending our time did not matter in the slightest to us? And if we don't, how blinding and binding do we make the stresses of the day when not so long ago it was air, having no form or recognition?

Where is the border of responsibility and sensuousness? What is it we must do and what is it that should be followed reverently in pursuit and curiosity, and where is the line?

Do we think often enough about how close we are — at all times — to thoughts of substance that can take us away from the *blind bind* and act as a waterslide conduit to some other realm of interaction? We are a moment's pause away, a stepping out from the status quo, to an undercurrent of intrigue.

Curiosity and mystery, whimsical wonder; these things erupted from your eyes the moment you opened them. And you give them out through the magic of memory long after you leave. There is simply no excuse worthy of eluding us from the responsibility to remember our requirement toward the occasionally irresponsible. The stepping away and in. Toward the realm that is not *productive*, but shakes and scurries us in the direction of the satisfaction that comes with the *imagined*. The *could be*.

The initial date of contact was found and the paperwork was filed and the day went on. Phone calls were made and meetings were had and the clock switched from 4:59 to 5:00 p.m. and the coat went on and the office light turned off and the door locked and the car started and the work ceased.

And a bloom happened.

A thought that was not relevant or pertinent latched itself onto the day and yielded conversation and curiosity. Is there anything more needed for us humans that constantly seem to be pulling away from each other and from the earth than conversation and curiosity?

The beneficial is not always the productive and the other way around; but I'm convinced that nestled within any moment is the possibility for *bloom*, and *bloom* is the possibility of letting more than what *needs* to be occurring, occur.

For the sake of being human. For the sake of reaching beyond the realm of what is expected. Finding whatever might be found there. Not knowing what that might be, being, perhaps, the entire point of the practice. The pursuit of possibility.

Images of Norway

Have you ever seen Norway?

I think to ask the question as my client appears to be reverting to what is, for her, a regular cycle—feeling overwhelmed and incapable of making headway to better her situation. Each time she identifies a problem she wants to work on, she stacks yet another problem on top of it, creating a list so long or convoluted, she forgets her initial goal. I work in housing case management with individuals who formerly experienced homelessness. These patterns are not uncommon, but this client reverts to this cycle of feeling incapable more often than most.

She is older, has a disability, and believes everyone is out to get her. And she has just told me, in the midst of listing the sabotaging situations, that her grandma and grandpa came through Ellis island from Norway. Our conversations are often scatter plots. This little nugget seemed a good place to cycle back to the humanness of things.

What was that? She asked, not hearing my original question.

Norway — where your ancestors are from. Have you ever seen pictures of it?

No, I don't think I have.

I spent hours on Google Earth as a kid, and I knew Norway was a hot spot for beauty. Fjords and fishing villages, the northern lights and snowcapped peaks. I pulled out my phone and Googled images of Norway. I showed them to my client. The first was a photo of a fjord from above, with a large boat cruising the light blue water below.

Oh WOW. Beautiful, she gasped.

The next one showed the Northern Lights. Suddenly her eyes, often urgent and bouncing back and forth, are locked on my screen. They are wide and glistening.

Oh wow wow WOW. BEAUTIFUL, just beautiful.

A few more, to the same response.

I spoke up, *that's where your ancestors are from! Isn't that cool? You may have relatives in that little fishing village. Who's to say?*

Do you know what they do in Norway? She asked.

I know they are big fishers. At least that's what I've read.

Well that explains it! I had my fishing license every year as a girl. I loved fishing!

Pretty cool how we are built from where they come from, I add.

Thank you. Thank you for showing me that.

Images of Norway broke through a narrative of incapability and of being overwhelmed. And I know this client — those feelings will come back. They did even as we sat there together. That's the harshness of trauma. Beauty doesn't solve it. But it does start rebuilding other narratives on top of it. Each time she began feeling incapable, I kindly and jovially said, remember Norway. And she agreed. And we got a few things accomplished. And — two people from drastically different worlds — we shared that brief and glorious feeling that bridges all voids between despair and possibility... wonder.

And now... a perhaps unnecessary riff on where this takes my mind... built on occupation, upbringing, and the domineering presence of narrow-minded religious ideology in the west...

We are here for a while and then for a while longer we aren't, and then a little while later we show up as something else from the matter we were before finding new form and function. And while we are here in this current life, we dip ourselves into little pockets — emotional states that characterize our experience of this little life we lead. But sometimes pockets become trenches. And we meander for miles in places of despair and darkness, seemingly digging ourselves deeper and deeper.

But what happens if we remember Norway? Remember that beyond the void of despair, there is beauty. Remember that there are pelicans flying in sync over Pacific blue, like, RIGHT NOW! Remember that there are whale babies following their whale mothers beneath that shimmering blue. Remember that there are trees that entwine their roots with the those of their offspring and send them nutrients, like a mother with baby to her breast. This is all going on! Right now! As you read this! Let's all pause and...

breathe
it
in

I'm so wildly unconvinced that this place is bad, that Earth is fallen or broken or depraved. We are all projectors, seeing what we cast out.

This is not to shame the one in despair; we all need to be there and to sift through the muddy residue. But there is a remembrance, even in the darkest moments, that all can rise in new possibility. And it takes wonder — the willingness even in despair — to stare wide-eyed at images of Norway and receive the beauty and let it swirl and swim within you. Marinade and stew. And begin to inject the dark veins of such despair with vibrancy. Transfusing over time. Ultimately bringing us back to that whole and glorious state of light and levity and love we inherently are, and that this place inherently is.

Lichen

I am reading about lichens
and the way two organisms
a fungus and an alga
collaborate and converge
into one.

I am sitting in my backyard
the suns slants onto the page through the tree above
shadows from the leaves
bounce across the text and the paper
each piece of wind creating visual rhythm.
Taken by this, I am no longer reading.

This wind comes from somewhere
and the book, too
its pages
its thought
hundreds and thousands of lives entwined
often, nearly always, unknowingly.
The wind and its pace the same
passing over landscape and emerging through weather
pattern.

I can't fully quantify.

But I'm here and I'm sitting and I'm in it!

Are We Seeing This?

I am a part of it!
And I *am* it!
The way of the lichen and the alga —
of two becoming one —
is not that far fetched
when all becomes
Now.

Crossing Paths With a Dolphin

I just read a passage in *Where the Crawdads Sing* about dolphins following along in the wake of the protagonist's boat. I became immediately envious and I thought about the nearest dolphins to me in that immediate moment seated in Spokane and what it would take, perhaps, to be fortunate enough to encounter one. A crossing of my path with theirs.

Roughly a 7-hour drive.

Find a charter.

Pay $75-100.

Be uncertain on open water, as I always find myself.

Hope the captain knows what to look for.

Or hope the fisher who has taken me along happens to have their path cross paths with a dolphin.

If I were to rise from my chair, get into my car and ditch my life for this cause right in this moment, I know the rough blueprint of my travels. I can trace them on a map and see them visually in my mind. It piques my curiosity to think about the first dolphin I would see if I were to make this pilgrimage — if I were to head to the ocean and not leave until my eyes met its eyes…

Where in the water is that dolphin right now? What course and path and story would exist between now and our encounter?

In the interim between then and now, does it care for its young?

Is it cared for by its elders?

Are they *playing,* as I have read dolphins do?

What fish or plant or other living, creeping things does its path intersect with on its path toward intersecting with me?

And how about me? What would I see on the drive?

Would I camp in the Tillamook Forest? Would I see a pine marten?

Where would I have to stop to use the bathroom?

What snack would I get to alleviate the hunger pains of a 7-hour drive?

Who would I call along the way to inform of my quest? What music would accompany it?

There is never a shortage of curiosity to be had. And today I wondered about a dolphin's path and my path intersecting and I'll never know the answers to questions about wonders in this particular instance. But I'm still attempting to bask in the brilliance of the wonder all the same.

We exist! Are we making use of this time with the light on?

Mike Christie

The Lizard Question

My wife and I bought a house that is 110 years old—
over 4 times our age—and is the first house we have
ever bought. This is an interesting thing. To invest and
reside and make a home out of the home of so many
other people—people who have died or who have
moved on or who, in this houses' case, now live next
door as a neighbor. And speaking of interesting things,
how about that phrase? *Next door.* So simple and so dull
but so full of potential for what resides behind the
phrase — what resides behind that *next* door.

But back to *our* door, I think of the front door of
this house and its hinges and the infinite swinging
open-and-shut they have facilitated in response to all
the comings and goings. Comings and goings ranging
from exits whose next entrance would be accompanied
by a new life as a couple rushes to the hospital and
walks back through that door a few days later with baby
in tow. Maybe that will be us?

I think of that door and its endless hinge swinging
and the entrances of finality—the last entrance—as the
individual walking through would later die in the
upstairs bedroom in their sleep. The door has swung

open to groceries in bags with contents from soils and farms and trees. The earliest of grocery run farms and trees replaced to time by who-knows-what.

The door has been opened to friends not seen in years.

Slammed from arguments slowing tearing the house apart.

Opened to dogs that visit and dogs that stay.

So many stories and possibilities have walked in and out that door.

And then there are the floors and the sinks and the windows and all their infinite interactions with lives I will never know. Lives that are more dirt than skin somewhere.

And speaking of the sink… sure, maybe it's been replaced a few times, and sure, there are *three* of them, not as clean and structured as running with the narrative of *one;* but think of all the water that has serpentined from faucet to drain to pipe in those sinks! Think of all the places that water came from and went to. Rivers and lakes and sky. And how some of that water, somewhere along the continuum of that water's existence—which is a whole other story of breadth beyond belief— somewhere along the line, that water was licked up by a lizard! At least, probably… If we are honest with ourselves regarding the vast amount of water that's flowed through the sinks in this home over its 110-year history and the vast (if hidden and elusive) quantity of lizards in the world.

Some water that has been in my sink has also been slurped down the throat of an amphibian friend. And then, somehow, in some way over the last 110 years, that lizard-slurped water ended up back in our sink because water is always flowing from source to house and back to source again. And because of this—in a very real way but in a way buried beneath many layers —this house connects me to more life than my own life could ever connect me to during its limited breadth. And this house does so by simply standing firm and *here* and not roaming and staking itself in anything other than its place and purpose. It has held its ground, quite literally. Stone foundation and all. And it has witnessed the world that has come to it, a world vastly beyond my 25-year comprehension, by being faithful to its sliver and slice.

Where do we go that is more important than where we are right now? Sure, there are appointments and trips and loved ones to see. Sure, we need to move to grow and become. This is all good. But where do we go that is more important than *right now, right here?*

I believe this is what my house is whispering to me. I believe this is what it is saying in the windows and the sinks and the floorboards of infinite step and the doorways of endless coming and going.

Our bodies are houses with legs. Moving around and opening and receiving — if we so choose—

the world we occupy. Accumulating and characterized by time. And time is, quite simply, a multitude of presences characterized by the now they reside within. These *multitudes of now* are endless doorways opening the self to the world. Our sinks and our doors and our floors are all the pieces of us that interact with this life and rock called earth. All the water we drink and food we consume and earth we tread upon. By being planted in me, like my house to its earth, I converge with infinite variety and possibility.

Am I what I am, though? Can I be in the space of myself and be grounded enough to let that be the space housing these holy intersections? How often are there days when I push back on the notion of owning and loving and being who I am?

My house is not the most put together. My house holds the byproducts of a world that has had its say with me. And I've had it pretty damn good! But my house is still my house. Your house is still your house. I am still me. I do not need to be the most presentable, the most put together, to be what I am; to have access to the space in time and presence that I occupy.

Moment by moment. I am here, here is now.

I have stood on pebbled pacific shore. In doing so, I have balanced upon millions of years of churning within sea, finding form on land, my feet finding ground on it, all journeying to *now* together, *this, apart, connected.*

I have held eons in my hands as I scoop up those pebbles. I have traveled years beyond the span of human existence by holding hands with what a moment presented. I have slurped sinks full of water. Right alongside the lizard. I have converged with more than I will ever know.

We are one road at the intersection to the infinite. There is an endless unfurling of years and happenings spewing out in vibrant color.

The door hinge, the sink, the eyes, the breath, the faithfulness to the rooted self; they take us to a world far beyond what is accomplished from some self-deprecating reaching. You are who you are, your house is your house, and all that happens to either is story spanning well *before* and well *beyond* any recognition or form either hold as themselves.

Gallup, Gallivant and Greeting

My dog comes traipsing into the room and his nails emphasize each step of his four legs. Farewell, new floor! His eyes look at my eyes and he is steadfast in making his way toward me. I do not need to move in such a moment. I just sit and am intersected with it.

There is light where there is light and we do not need to move to intersect with it. It hits us and the space we occupy in varying quantities; shape shifting and reframing and re-revealing with each subtle movement we make. Or no movement. It moves and changes and exposes itself eternal.

Every day there is some moment. Obviously. Everyday there are some moments, large, small whatever, greeting and galloping and intersecting with whatever we are doing, wherever we are.

To not be inspired is not the same as to not be within. Inspiration ebbs and flows and that is fine and as it must be. But you are always cradled by creation. Creation needn't be some great artist, bearded and beyond. That's old news.

But instead, the unfolding of everything before you.

This is all we have. This is all anything is; gallop and gallivant and greeting.

The Water and the Rock

Every morning moisture rises from the water
droplets crash
against the rock cliff face of shoreline.
They shoot up
and litter the hard surface
with soft, gentle liquid.

What are the combinations
of the world that pair unlikely friends?
Could it be
that in all places
opposites
solids, liquids
hopes, fears
loves, hates
layer the same place?

Nothing in this life should come as a surprise
when every piece is a word to the story
that rolls right alongside us with every breath

Back on the shoreline the whispers of waves from the
Pacific
send off sprays that plume toward the rock
You will find your way back, they say.
To the rock or the water?

Second after second the water will dribble back in
year after the year so will the rock erode.
Varying time sequences
patterns the same
and what is a year to the ocean or the rock
but a brief blip in a season everlasting?

We can't escape interconnectivity
or oneness
we can only distract ourselves from it.
Our true being
the parts deep within
melt into the rest.
It's where we began
it is where we go.
So let's feel the bark of the tree as brother
the softly swaying grass as sister.
Let's lie down in the field of holistic being
and perhaps we'll find our worries
won't go away
but melt into the all.
Becoming as minute and unimpressive as a year
to the ocean and the rock.

My Grandma Hated My Long Hair

My grandmother used to look at my long hair with utter disdain, as if there was nothing more grotesque she could witness regarding a grandchild. And the 60-or-so-year gap between her and I shrouded her discontent with a certain level of respect on my part.

Love was always there. Support for hair styles... not so much.

She's gone now. To where? A mystery. And my hair is longer than it's ever been. And I wish so badly I could hear her tell me how much she hates it in the way she always did that, in the weird and wonderfully magic of the grandmotherly way, which also tells me how much love she has for me. The sly smile of her distaste. The subtle laughter. The, *did Gillette go on strike* comment she'd add as a quip if a beard was also at play.

But her voice is only an echo in memory's cavern and I wish for all I cannot *hold* any longer or *hear* any longer and I'm lost to time. Like all memory that shapes and molds.

Yet *here* you and I are. Alive. Built from what *was* and building what *will be*.

We are *now* just as *now* was *then* and *then* will be through what *now* has to say.

speak.

Andy Kaufman Yields the Bald Eagle Moment

It was a cold day but not *too* cold. It was also a day spent inside the house attempting to piece together thoughts. To then find the right words for and to transcribe. To then share for about 16.4 to 21.7 minutes later in the week on Sunday around 10:34 a.m. On such days there is inevitably such an elevated level of stir-craziness that 10:22 a.m. rolls around and the dog and I can't help but pick ourselves up, stretch out our legs, and bundle up for a neighborhood stroll.

His leash goes on. My coat and hat and gloves and extra wool socks and boots and sweater go on. The bundling because I have been on enough walks in this quarter of a life I've lived to know that having even the slightest inclination of *chill* is far worse than feeling warm and secure. All the prep work accomplished, we exit the house, slamming the door behind us four times —because the strike plate is coming off — and proceed to our route.

There are a multitude of paths we take, all arriving at the same location. For Oliver and me, that location is a bluff with trails carved alongside. It is there the dog can run free, and I can watch as the ponderosas cling to the sharp slope of the earth. It is there we can both rest atop a slight cliff and look at the creek that runs below, parallel to the train tracks; where we can gaze at the tiny farms only five minutes out of town that sit in this veiled little valley southwest of the city. In this space, we are overseers to happenings we don't know of, but witness, like the birds that often circle the sky above.

But in order to get to our favorite location, we have to decide which turn and twist and maneuver to take. And unlike the journeys of our previous home downtown, in this neighborhood there are no stoplights—only the flow and feet fumbling toward; trying to lend variety to the journey toward the known place with each pilgrimage.

Today we decide to take the northern of the two routes. After about 2,300 steps, we arrive at Cherry Street. Following the sidewalk until there is nothing left to follow, we empty onto a trail running alongside the neighborhood park. In the field beyond the playground is another dog and another dog's human playing fetch. I have on headphones and am listening to some podcast about caves and really want to keep it that way, but when the bubble-bellied, bristle-bearded, baby-boomer man and his doodle of a dog waddle toward us, both with jovial grins, it is clear I will be coming out from the caverns for a bit.

The man and I converse and he laughs and I laugh and we share thoughts about our favorite comedians and then he just full fledge *dives in*. He talks about …

the power of comedy and the comedy *I* (he) heard on the radio as a kid and how *you* (me) never had to *deal* with *that* and how Robin Williams was a troubled man but the best soul you ever met although *I* (he) never met him and although *I* (he) have heard otherwise and Jim Carey!… whatever happened *THERE* but *gosh* talk about another *genius* and Andy Kaufman I mean you talk about a *FIREBRAND* no way around that one, no way whatsoever.

As he talks, I shyly and delicately brush away the intermittent spit that has spewed from between his right canine and right lateral incisor and has soared across the chilled morning air onto my face and I smile and I nod and I add what I can and I say something about how …

comedy helps people become *unfurled* and Lord knows we need more of *that* both in terms of us becoming that way and the world around us becoming that way because it's just too damn cold!

This is all well and good, but after about 20 minutes or so, Oliver and I are ready to set out for our destination. I was ready to see the creek and its flow alongside the train tracks and their invitation toward movement and the bluff and ponderosa and all the other pieces tied to that spot. The conversation ceased slowly. Because even if I want to carry on with whatever I am doing, it is impossible for me to end conversations with strangers.

Bristle-beard gave Oliver one final treat and we parted ways and shook hands and nodded and did every other thing possible to delay an interaction from ending because clearly neither of us really knew how one does that.

The walk continued. The monotony set back in. The headphones and the podcast went back on. The mind drifted back to the world of caves. And the feet and the paws plopped one in front of the other. And we arrived at our spot. An arrival simultaneous with another.

Queue whimsy.

I would like to imagine that at the same time that the bristle-beard and I were conversing, there was a bald eagle much deeper south; somewhere amidst the bluff and its labyrinth landscape. Swooping and soaring and occasionally making its way down toward the creek to look for something to eat. Likely it was following a course only it knew and was letting itself do so fluidly. Perhaps it perched on a few different branches? Saw some other critters and said 'hello' to them? Or maybe it even got stuck in a conversation with a hawk that just couldn't help but boast about some catch it had made the other day — in such a way as to try and compare itself to the ways of the eagle and come across as credible and competent? To which the eagle, polite and courteous, nodded and acknowledged the catch all the while patiently waiting for the right moment to soar away from such shallow conversations centering around the unspoken insecurity that all hawks deal with? Who knows? But why not consider such things a possibility, right?

Anyways… Oliver and I had stopped in our spot to look at the creek, and just as we stopped, swooping over our heads from behind us came a large and imposing shadow, followed quickly by its physical form.

A bald eagle sailed in the sky directly in front of where we had arrived to sit and gaze. And this eagle didn't fly away, it seemed to deem the spot worthy of some extra time, just as we did. It circled the exact scope of my peripheral vision. And it did so 7 times. No wing flaps. Simple soaring. And Oliver and I, some 20 or so minutes behind schedule, both sat and gazed. Right on time.

Whatever it was the eagle was doing the past 30 minutes had intersected with whatever Oliver and I had happened to be doing for the previous 30 minutes and whatever it was that made bristle-beard want to riff on Andy Kaufman. And, in a real stretch of this flight of fancy, the fact that Andy Kaufman was alive and existed well before me and chose to live the life he lived… it all, in a way, led to me and this bald eagle sharing space. And I can't help but be curious about all that's tied to that.

Burble

The water is
burbling and bursting forth
in every moment where a simple blade of grass
becomes an entity worth praise.

All is a gate
swung wide open in welcome
urging us into the place of mind
that sees no distinction between holy and otherwise.

This may seem so far from here —
beyond the realm of reason and norm —
but flick off the filter of flaccid form.
Awaken
to the that which is already singing
muted only by the mind
with its gate closed.

The Light Behind

A client was in my office after a housing contingency plan. A meeting where property management, kindly, but firmly, let her know that any more lease violations could lead to termination of her housing. The housing that got her off the street. She's in my office now. There's a punctuated silence. But it breaks:

"It feels like someone has sucked the joy out of me. I can't find joy anymore," she says through tears.

Her head is down. She is far away.

We are on the phone with DSHS, trying to resolve one of the many stressors that have created this feeling. There is a long hold, as there always seems to be.

"You lived in Arkansas for a bit, right?" I ask.

Attempting to move away from burdensome task into reflective memory.

She says "yes." And she begins to tell me about living there. I mention I've been to Arkansas. Seen the hot springs and the hills of the Ozarks. I ask her where she is from. She tells me of the place, its name. How it is hidden by those hills. She rolls her wheelchair over to my computer. We go on Google Maps and I look up the town. There are about five north/south streets, six east/west. It is small. It is one you have to zoom in quite a bit to see. One with likely less than 5,000 people. One where people undoubtedly remember her name. And think of her. And her role there, in that little slice of place.

On the map, I can see there's a fly shop in the town. Striking, given its limited variety of businesses and minimal population. There are flies on my Orvis sweater. We laugh at the connection and she tells me about the serpentine river full of trout. It's the geographic marker of the area and it runs through the middle of town. I can see this. Satellite imagery accompanies memory and story as she tells me how she used to go to the park it ran beside and bask on the shore. Near the railroad bridge. Under the trees.

She asks to do street view. At her direction, we start in the center of the town and make our way out toward the perimeter. As we virtually cruise, we pass by a coffee stand. A store to rent kayaks.

We are still on hold.

"Keep going," she says.

The pavement turns to dirt. More and more trees overhang. Blue skies overhead on the screen. Moments before we had talked about clouds and Seasonal Affective Disorder.

"Wait, wait! Go back."

On the dirt road sits an old house.

"There's my old Mercedes! Oh my! This is from a while back! This is from when I lived there!"

A vintage old car sits in front. She tells me about the place. A house on a slight incline. Stone foundation, beautiful old stone wall out front. Possibly late 1800s. Trees and vegetation surround. Grill in the front yard. Life. Happiness. A home. Her old Rottweiler she says, buried under "that tree there" as she points.

And there's laughter all of a sudden. Smiles all of a sudden.

Still on hold.

"My daughter is a surgeon there. In a small hospital in the neighboring town that's slightly bigger. She and her husband have two daughters."

An unfurling has happened. A reminder of the beauty and light and story inherently woven within. More than the stress. More than the heavy. We are people. No matter the clouds that linger, always light behind.

Mike Christie

Story Started

The universe was birthed by a bang
Some say cosmic energy
Some say a booming voice
The truth is obviously the same…

A story started.

Somewhere along that timeline existed the spiked
dinosaurs!
Why have such things lost the wonder they held in our
youth?

I'm not sure I understand.

Mike Christie

Acknowledgments

There are a lot of individuals to thank for this project!
Thank you to all of you who have purchased this book
and made it to this point. For reading and hopefully
laughing and thinking and participating with what I
have put on these pages.

Thank you to Emily, for supporting me and rooting for
me and for encouraging me that putting these thoughts
down is good and deserves space and time. And thank
you for being there. The endless walks, sometimes with
words, sometimes not.

Thank you to Oliver for needing walks and forcing me
to get off my butt and see *stuff* and for providing a
springboard time and time again to hilarity and
meaningfulness just by being himself.

Thank you Colin, Catherine, Jack, Dad and Mom for
being a biological and spiritual and familial unit that
encourages and celebrates each other. For being there
and for laughing and not laughing and for helping
shape the filter I see through.

Thank you to Vanessa for the amazing cover design
and the way your art portrays such lush abundance!
Can't wait for the Wildland Coop and so encouraged

and inspired by all that you and Michael do for the Spokane community.

Thank you Steven Rodgers for editing this book. We've never met each other and perhaps never will, but your hand and skill is all over the words here. I like thoughts… but I'm not all that skilled with grammar. I'm indebted to you!

Thanks to all my friends who are willing to grab a beer or a coffee or go to a John Craigie show or WHATEVER for being there and creating a web of support I know I can always rely and fall back on. In a lot of ways, we are built from the people we are with, I sense. I'm so grateful for all those who choose to walk with me.

Thanks to my neighborhood for the trees and landscape that speaks a multitude of different stories. I'm just trying to be here enough to listen!

Thanks to those who can't be named for HIPPA reasons for resiliency and authenticity.

Thank you to frogs, snails, moss, etc.

Thank you to the nameless flow-like thing weaving together all observation and things with *thingness toward* one another. At least I hope that's happening. Who care's what name it goes by. But yeah… thanks!

About the Author

Mike, in the words of his late hero Brian Doyle, is a story catcher. Someone on the lookout for meaning and levity. He is a pastor at All These Branches, a progressive spirit community. He is a care coordinator with Catholic Charities. A husband to Emily. A dog dad to Ollie. And a friend to many. A fan of beer, moss, frogs, snails, mushrooms; amongst other things; residing in Spokane, WA.

mikechristie.net
insta: @m.christie

www.ingramcontent.com/pod-product-compliance
Lightning Source LLC
Chambersburg PA
CBHW050236270326
41914CB00034BA/1938/J